Waiting- Patiently, Expectantly

Heather Varon

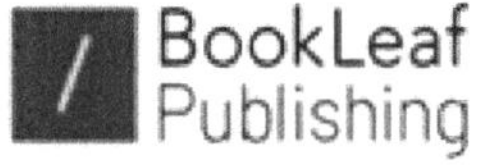
BookLeaf Publishing

Presentation by *BookLeaf Publishing*

Web: www.bookleafpub.com

E-mail: info@bookleafpub.com

ISBN: 9789357210386

First edition 2022

DEDICATION

To my sweet Sophia Kate...may you always feel loved.

ACKNOWLEDGEMENT

A huge thank you to my tribe...you have been with me at my highest and my lowest...and you all love me no matter what!

Waiting

heart broken
shattered into tiny pieces
waiting...
patiently, expectantly
to be put back together
with a soft touch
a gentle kiss
a kind word
longing for intimacy
waiting...
patiently...
expectantly...
waiting...
for the one

Trust

2

Trust
Handing it over
Full faith that everything will work out
Maybe not exactly what you want
But even bigger and better
Than you ever imagined
That's the gift of hope
Trust

Collection of Love

A heart leaf
Purple Wildflower
Bits of grass
A long weed
Pebbles and rocks
Thin sticks
A collection of love
To bring the outside…
Inside

Answered Prayer

Bright blue eyes
That shine like the galaxy
Long flowing blonde hair
Pink rosy cheeks
With a smile that lights up a room
And a laugh that's contagious
A sweet answered prayer

Fighting Fear

Plunging deeper, darker
Can't breathe
Chest tight
Holding my breath
Waiting…
For the next move
When will it come
What will it hold
Fear gripping, squeezing
Fighting to let go
Be strong…
And courageous
Not alone
Gasping for air
Gulping for relief
Holding my hand
Don't let go
Fighting to hold on

Make It Stop

Falling tears
Onto my pillow
Heaving chest
Out of breath
Spinning thoughts
Out of control
Asking...why now?
Over and over
Feeling lost, lonely
Make it stop

Moving On

Moving On
Letting Go
Feeling empty inside
What once lit a fire
Slowly faded away
Hollow, shallow
Heart stopped beating
Dead inside

Rollercoaster

Ups and downs
Twists and turns
Stomach in knots
Wake up feeling excited
Almost giddy
Euphoric
Hopeful for the future
Then an upset
A wrong turn
A misstep
Excitement turns to overthinking
Anxiety takes over
Mind races
Long, sleepless nights
Unsure, uncertain
Fearful for what's next
A toxic cycle
Break the chains
Dig into the Truth
Trust in the future

Courage

Take risks
Open your heart
Abundant love
Ready to give
Ready to receive
A revival of the spirit
Take flight
Have courage

Emptiness

Pit in stomach
Hollowed chest
Heart pounding
Deep breaths
Eerily quiet…while
Spiraling thoughts
Threaten to take over
Emptiness fills the future
Suffocating hope

But God

...But God
Tips His hand
Ever so slightly
Blows a gentle breeze
Across my cheek
Sends a butterfly
To flutter its delicate wings
Onto my palm
Whispers softly
Into my ear
I have a plan for you
You are not alone
Your heart is filled
With my love
Sit with me
Be very still
For I am
With you
My spirit is stronger
Than what you are facing
My God…
Is with me
I am not alone

In the Stillness

12

You whisper my name
Feel your heart beating
A touch of your hand
On the small of my back
A kiss on my lips
Soft and sweet
Melting into your arms
Fitting together
As if made for each other
In the stillness
Of the night

Quiet

My mind
Slows down
Inhale…
Exhale
My pulse
Steadies
Inhale…
Exhale
My jaw
Relaxes
Inhale…
Exhale
My fists
Unclench
Inhale…
Exhale
My eyes
Close
Inhale…
Exhale
All is quiet

Salty

No response
24 hours later
So many issues
Can't be just one
Pulling and pushing
Too many forces
Fear of commitment
Fear of regret
As it lingers
No longer sweet
But a bit salty

Shining

A light wind
Rustles the leaves
The brilliant sun shines
Brightly across the grass
Songbirds sweetly sing
Far into the distance
A woodpecker pecks
At a hollow tree
Love radiates outwardly
Glowing with hope and forever
Shining brightly like the sun

Healing

A moment in time
When you realize
Your heart is softened
It's ready
No bitterness remains
Peace reverberates
Creating a glow
Flushed cheeks
A smile that reaches the eyes
No hastened steps
Just honoring where you are
A moment in time

Journey

Time marches on
Flying by
Seasons change
People change
Nothing is the same
Everything is new and different
Challenging
Peaks and valleys
Tears shed for time lost
Time wasted
Peace returns
Filling the mind, heart, and soul
The journey continues
A daily process
Renewing the spirit

Running

Away from the past
Far from bad choices
Fast from mistakes
Charging ahead
Into the future
Not recognizing the present
Missing moments
Wishing days away
Trying to stay ahead
Steadying the pace
Life's a marathon
Not a sprint

Awakening

Heaviness...
Nothingness...
Stillness...
Hopelessness...
All fading beneath the surface;
Threatening to overstay their welcome
Pushing past the awkwardness of silence
Making a way for hope
Spreading wings of independence
Stepping into freedom
Breaking chains of the past
Awakening into a new spirit
Trusting better days ahead
Choosing peace instead of fear

Transformation

Separated into two
Causing chaos
But catching my breath
Settling into a rhythm
As my path changes
Ever so slightly
From what I dreamed
Forming a new present
An unknown future
Out of my control
Inhaling peace while
Exhaling relief
What was meant to undo me
Has transformed me
Made me stronger
Not where I thought I'd be
Challenging patterns
Tackling demons
Creating an awareness
Self-reflection, self-care, self-love
Knowing I was made for more
Connecting on so many levels
Right time...
Right place

The One

Watching the majestic moon
Shine her magical powers
Over the darkness
Promising, trusting, hoping
A sea of gold
Illuminating
A bright future
Outlasting the darkness
Out of the depths
A magnetic force…so
Powerful…
Forceful…
Unstoppable…
Her passion attracts
The one

ABOUT THE AUTHOR

Heather Varon lives in the DFW area with her daughter Sophia and puppy Pearl. She has been in education for 25 years. When she has free time, she loves to run, read, do yoga, and travel.

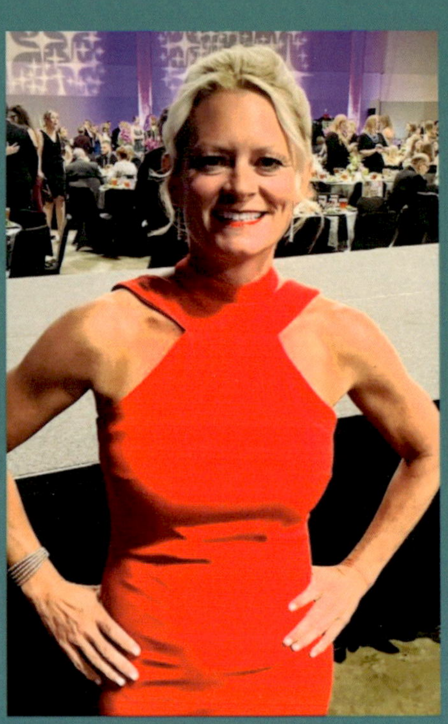

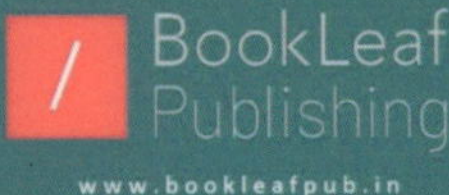

IMANI MINER

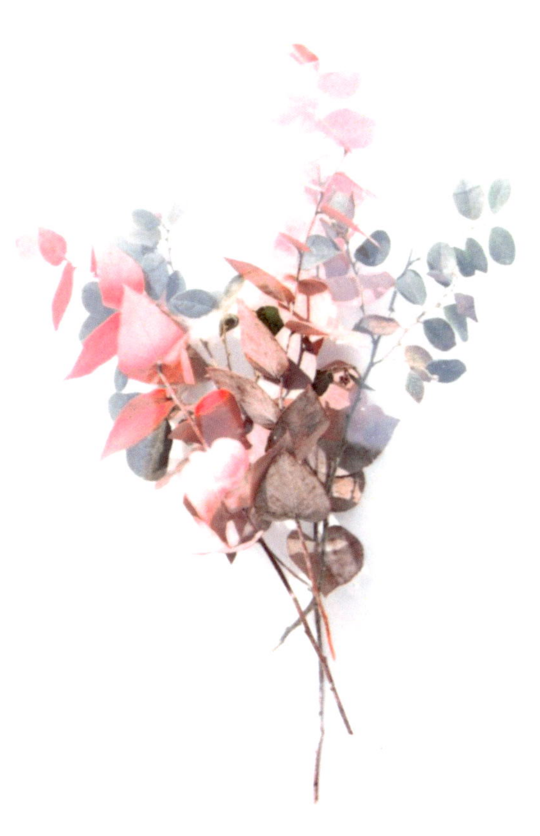

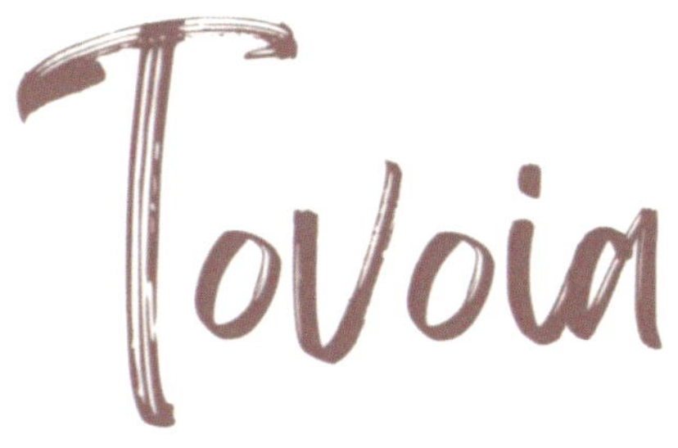

Tovoia